GEARED FOR GROWTH BIBLE STUDIES

CONTROLLED BY LOVE

A STUDY IN 2 CORINTHIANS

BIBLE STUDIES TO IMPACT THE LIVES OF ORDINARY PEOPLE

Written by Dorothy Russell

The Word Worldwide

CHRISTIAN FOCUS

For details of our titles visit us on our website
www.christianfocus.com

ISBN 1-84550-022-9

Copyright © WEC International

10 9 8 7 6 5 4 3 2 1

Published in 2005 by
Christian Focus Publications Ltd, Geanies House,
Fearn, Tain, Ross-shire, IV20 ITW, Scotland
and
WEC International, Bulstrode, Oxford Road,
Gerrards Cross, Bucks, SL9 8SZ

Cover design by Alister MacInnes

Printed and bound by Bell & Bain, Glasgow

CONTENTS

QUESTIONS AND NOTES

ANSWER GUIDE

PREFACE
GEARED FOR GROWTH

'Where there's LIFE there's GROWTH: Where there's GROWTH there's LIFE.'

WHY GROW a study group?

Because as we study the Bible and share together we can

- learn to combat loneliness, depression, staleness, frustration, and other problems
- get to understand and love each other
- become responsive to the Holy Spirit's dealing and obedient to God's Word

and that's GROWTH.

How do you GROW a study group?

- Just start by asking a friend to join you and then aim at expanding your group.
- Study the set portions daily (they are brief and easy: no catches).
- Meet once a week to discuss what you find.
- Befriend others, both Christians and non-Christians, and work away together

see how it GROWS!

WHEN you GROW ...

This will happen at school, at home, at work, at play, in your youth group, your student fellowship, women's meetings, mid-week meetings, churches and communities,

you'll be REACHING THROUGH TEACHING.

INTRODUCTORY STUDY

You get into your car, and start up the engine. Nothing happens.	What is wrong?	You have run out of petrol. There is no POWER.

OR

You stop at a friend's house, leave the engine running and forget to put on the brake.	What happens?	The car runs downhill by itself and crashes! There is NO ONE IN CONTROL.

Is your life like this? No power to serve God effectively. No one in control of your life.

In 2 Corinthians, Paul gives us the key to living a satisfying life:

The love of Christ controls us.... He died for all, that those who live might live no longer for themselves, but for Him, who for their sake died and was raised' (2 Cor. 5:14, 15.)

Will you learn these verses by heart, as we go into the study of this heart-warming epistle? They show us the true motivation for living.

Outside the big mission centre at Mvumi, Tanzania (made famous by the Jungle Doctor books) was a large notice showing the direction of the hospital, nursing school, midwifery training, girls' school, laboratory training school, and hospital stores. So many facilities were made available for the local people by a Christian mission! And set clearly in the centre of the board is the explanation –

'THE LOVE OF CHRIST CONTROLS US'

Can you explain why the text outside Mvumi hospital is the key to Christian missions, and indeed to Christian living?

Check your own motives:

Why do you go to church?
Why do you show kindness to others?

How do you make your decisions?
What determines what you do in your leisure time?
What is the purpose of your life?

When we know what Christ wants us to do, and have the right motivation for doing it, we then need the power to do it. Make Philippians 3:10 your prayer – 'That I may know Him, and the **power** of His resurrection'.

2 Corinthians is a very personal letter. In it, the apostle Paul opens his very heart to us. He does not methodically expound the gospel, but he gives us glimpses of the way in which he, a new man in Christ **lives** the gospel.

Two great themes which we shall meet within this letter, are – 'Christ in Control' and 'The Power of Christ'.

Commentators agree that it is not easy to trace the sequence of thought in this letter so we shall content ourselves with digging out the gems, rather than tracing a vein of gold from beginning to end.

Do refer to more than one version of the Bible if possible.

BACKGROUND NOTES to 2 Corinthians

In Acts 18 we read of Paul's first visit to Corinth. After he had spent eighteen months there, we read that Gallio became proconsul, and the trouble started! As we know from secular history that Gallio took office in AD 51, we can date the founding of the Corinthian church accurately. About five years later (AD 56), the letter we know as '2 Corinthians' was written.

Paul left Ephesus (Acts 20:1) in great distress over problems at Corinth, hoping to meet up with Titus at Troas and get up-to-date news of the Corinthian Church. However, when he arrived at Troas, although he had opportunity to preach the gospel there, he didn't stay long, as Titus hadn't arrived (2 Cor. 2:12, 13) and he was still anxious. In this frame of mind he pressed on to Macedonia, and to his joy, met Titus there. He was further encouraged and relieved by the news which Titus brought about the Christians in Corinth. (2 Cor. 7:5-7)

This, then, is the background to the writing of this letter, and we shall notice Paul's deep concern for his fellow-Christians as we read it. Indeed, he wrote it so that they would become mature Christians (2 Cor. 12:19 and 13:9, Living Bible).

Paul visited Corinth again some months after this letter was written, as he planned, (2 Cor. 12:14) and while he stayed there ministering to the people in person, he wrote the letter to the Romans.

CYPRUS

ASIA

EPHESUS

TROAS

CRETE

MACEDONIA

ACHAIA

CORINTH

ITALY

SICILY

STUDY 1

SUFFERING AND COMFORT

QUESTIONS

DAY 1   *Chapter 1:1-7.*
a) In what three ways is God described in verse 3?

b) Why does God comfort us?

c) Have you proved the truth of this? (Isa. 49:13)

DAY 2   *Chapter 1:3-10.*
a) Compare verse 5 with verse 7. What point is Paul making here?

b) How does Paul describe his own sufferings in Asia? (v. 8) Read 2 Corinthians 4:8, 9; 6:4-10 and 11:24-28.

DAY 3   *Chapter 1:8-11.*
a) What did Paul's sufferings force him to do? (Prov. 3:5)

b) What did he ask the Christians at Corinth to do? (2 Cor. 1:11)

DAY 4   *Chapter 1:12-14.*
a) What was Paul able to say about himself with complete honesty?

b) Can you say this?

c) To what did he attribute the ability to live a life like that? (I Cor. I5:I0)

DAY 5   *Chapter I:I5-22. (Read in the Living Bible, if possible)*
a) What does Paul say men of the world do?

b) Are you ever like this? (v. I7)

c) Verse 20. Can you think of three promises of God that have been fulfilled in Jesus?

DAY 6   *Chapter I:23–Chapter 2:4.*
a) What reason does Paul give for not visiting the Corinthians at that time?

b) How do we know that Paul found it difficult to write and rebuke his fellow Christians (in a previous letter)? See Acts 20:3I.

DAY 7   *Chapter 2:5-II.*
a) What should the Christian's approach be to one who has done wrong? (Matt. 6:I4, I5)

b) How has Paul been able to forgive the wrongdoer, and why has he done this?

NOTES

There is a pattern for Christian living which emerges from the verses we have been studying. It is this:

Christ suffered (He is an example for us)	*We suffer* (we are an example for others)	*Others suffer* (we help others by our example)
God comforts us.	We are comforted.	We comfort others.
We suffer.	We rely on God for help	Our behaviour testifies to others.

Can you see how, as Christians, our lives are bound up with God, (we need Him so much), and with other people (they are influenced by the way we react)?

Jesus said 'Abide in Me, and I in you' and, 'Love one another as I have loved you' (John 15:4, 12).

This is the essence of Christianity, and it links up with the theme of our study – 'The Love of Christ controls us'.

Let's look at Paul's life, as portrayed here:

1. Afflicted and crushed, to the point of death (2 Cor. 1:8).
2. He sees the reason – to make him rely, not on himself but on God (1:9). ('Man's extremity is God's opportunity.')
3. He finds that it works! (1:10)
   The Psalms are full of the experiences of others who have found this too, e.g. Psalm 34:4-6; 46:1; 43:5; 107:6, 13, 19, 28.
4. He can honestly say his life is marked by 'holiness and godly sincerity' (2 Cor. 1:12).
5. An indication of this is that he says what he means, and means what he says (1:18, 19). (How can he do otherwise, with Christ in control?)
6. He is considerate of others, and sensitive to their feelings (1:23).
7. He has a Christ-like love for others (2:4).
8. He is forgiving (2:10).
9. He is very much aware of the spiritual warfare that is going on (2:11).

STUDY 2

LIKENESS TO CHRIST

QUESTIONS

DAY 1   *Chapter 2:12, 13.*
See also 'Background Notes', page 4.
a) Whom had Paul hoped to find when he came to Troas?

b) Read through Paul's letter to this man, found later on in the New Testament. What impresses you about it?

DAY 2   *Chapter 2:14-17.*
a) Can you explain how verse 14 supports Paul's two great themes in this letter? (Christ in control, and the power of Christ.)

b) According to verse 15, what is the purpose of a Christian's life? Are you doing this?

DAY 3   *Chapter 3:1-3.*
a) What did Paul mean by saying the Christians were like letters from Christ? Compare verse 3 with Exodus 31:18; Jeremiah 31:33 and Ezekiel 36:26.

b) What was the difference between the old covenant and the new?

DAY 4   *Chapter 3:4-6.*
a) What made Paul so confident about his ministry (see 12:9)?

b) Why does he say that 'the letter kills' (NIV), 'the written code kills' (RSV), 'the old way ends in death' (LB)? Read these verses in the Living Bible, and also Romans 7:9, 10.

DAY 5 *Chapter 3:7-11 and Exodus 34:28-35.*
a) How was the 'splendour' or 'glory' of the old covenant evident to the people?

b) What can be deduced about the 'splendour' or 'glory' of the new covenant?

DAY 6 *Chapter 3:12-18.*
a) Something caused Moses to veil his face (vv. 7, 13) and the opposite made Paul bold and frank in his ministry (vv. 11, 12). What was it?

b) What is meant by 'a veil lies over their minds' or 'their hearts are blind' in verses 14, 15?

c) When is the veil taken away?

DAY 7 *Verse 18 (Read this over and over to get the full implication for yourself).*
a) In what ways can you and I 'behold' (or 'reflect') the glory of the Lord?

b) What happens to us when we do this constantly? Look up Romans 12:2 and Matthew 17:2 where the same word is used. Read Exodus 34:29 again. Do not proceed further till after your discussion.

NOTES

Now read these comments.

The thread that runs through our study this week is that human beings can become like God! Not the age-old, yet very up-to-date idea that man has 'come of age' and can do without God (Gen. 3:5), but rather that, depending completely on Him, we can be transformed into His likeness. This is the work of the Spirit of God, and is brought out in our study by a series of contrasts.

Christians are 'living letters'

a) not written with pen and ink – but by the Spirit (2 Cor. 3:3).

b) not engraved on stone (Exod. 31:18) – but written on the heart (Jer. 31:33).

God's new law

a) is not written rules	but of the Spirit (v. 6).
b) The old law condemns	but the Spirit gives life.
c) The old law came with splendour.	The Spirit came with greater splendour (v. 8).
d) Moses wore a veil.	Christ takes the veil away (v. 14).
e) When the Jews hear the law, their minds are veiled.	When a man turns to the Lord, the veil is taken away (v. 16).

So, with His life-giving Spirit at work in our hearts, and the veil removed through Christ, we can – 'turn our eyes upon Jesus, and look full in His wonderful face.'

As we do this day by day, we have His promise that we shall actually be changed more and more into His likeness.

What a tremendous thought!

Consider the words used in different translations of verse 18 for this process...

'... we all ... are being changed into his likeness...' (RSV).

'But we ... become more and more like him' (LB).

'We are constantly being transfigured into His very own image' (Amplified).

'... that same glory ... transforms us into His likeness...' (GNB).

'... we are transfigured into his likeness...' (NEB).

'And we ... are being transformed into his likeness...' (NIV).

The same word is used in Matthew 17:2, where Christ's whole person shone on the Mount of Transfiguration.

We should ask ourselves two questions after a study like this:

1. Do I want to be changed, or do I take my particular faults as being 'just me'?

2. Am I more like Christ today than I was a year ago? Six months ago? Last week?

A verse to learn – chapter 3:18.

v 4 the god of this age
Eph 6:12 our struggle is... against the powers of this dark world
& against the spiritual forces of evil in the heavenly realms

Heb6:5 who have tasted the
goodness of the word of God
and the powers of the coming
age
Jesus - Rev 15:3
  King of the ages
            plural

Rev 12:1 - 13:1
Jn 12:31 Now is the time for judgment on this world. now the
          prince of this world will be driven out.

STUDY 3

HUMAN WEAKNESS AND DIVINE POWER

QUESTIONS

- Yes because of my sin.

DAY 1 *Chapter 4:1-6.*
Are you ever discouraged in Christian witness?
a) Why does Paul say he 'does not lose heart', 'never gives up', 'does not get discouraged'?   because of God's mercy

b) What was 'the truth' that is referred to in verse 2? (see v. 5).

v 4 the gospel of the Glory of christ   v 5 Jesus christ as Lord

DAY 2 *Chapter 3:12-16, Chapter 4:3-4.*
a) Why is it that many people who hear the gospel remain unbelievers?

(see Mark 4:15)

b) How does the Bible describe such people? (2 Cor. 4:3-4)

DAY 3 *Chapter 4:4-6.*
a) What can you discover about God from verse 6 and Genesis 1:3?

b) Read Acts 26:13-15. Might Paul have been thinking of this occasion?

c) What does verse 6 mean in your own experience?

DAY 4 *Chapter 4:7.*
a) What is the 'treasure' Paul refers to?

QUESTIONS (contd.)

b) Why does God entrust this to us? (Acts 9:15)

c) Why is God able to use weak human beings like us in this way? (2 Cor. 12:9)

DAY 5   *Chapter 4:8-12.*
a) Which parts of these verses show human weakness and which Divine power?

b) Compare verses 8 and 11 with Galatians 2:20.

DAY 6   *Chapter 4:13-15.*
a) Why can Paul have peace of mind even in the face of danger and death? (see 5:8.)

b) What great demonstration of God's power did the apostles often refer to in the New Testament? verse 14; Acts 2:24, 32; 3:15; 4:10, etc.

DAY 7   *Chapter 4:16-18.*
a) In what ways can the Christian's 'inner nature' or 'inner self' be renewed every day? (Col. 3:1, 2, 10)

b) What is the difference between material things and spiritual things?

c) Which should be more important to us? (Matt. 10:28)

NOTES

Let's look at this together.

We have been reading about two kinds of human weakness in this chapter – (1) Spiritual weakness; (2) Physical weakness.

(1) Spiritual

In our ministry of Christian witness (2 Cor. 4:1), (translated 'this wonderful work of telling his Good News to others' in the LB), it is easy to get discouraged.

We try so hard to share our faith with others, and so often they don't understand.

Why is this? It is because a mighty spiritual conflict is going on all the time, for the eternal souls of men.

Compare verses 4 and 6.

Verse 4	Verse 6
'the god of this world'	'the God who said, '"Let light shine"'
(prince of darkness)	(God, who is Light)
this god blinds	this God shines
he works in the minds of unbelievers,	He has shone in our hearts,
he keeps them from seeing the light.	He gives the light of the gospel.

What can we do?

Some give up (v. 1). Some try psychological techniques (v. 2). This passage tells us we must declare 'the truth openly' (v. 2 NEB) and 'proclaim Christ Jesus as Lord' (v. 5 NEB).

Sharing Christ with others is the God-appointed means by which the devil is defeated, human beings turn to the Lord, and He shines in their hearts (see I Cor. 1:21.)

(2) Physical

Paul says of himself in I Corinthians 2:3, 'I was with you in weakness, and in much fear and trembling' when he spoke for Christ. Have you ever felt like this?
Humanly speaking, he was unimpressive, and was apparently no orator (2 Cor. 10:10).

He had a physical affliction, which he called a 'thorn in the flesh' (2 Cor. 12:7), which was a constant trial to him.

Do you suffer from shyness? a physical handicap? nerves? headaches? a physical illness? an inferiority complex?

If you do, then read 2 Corinthians 12:8-10 and PRAISE THE LORD! because God chooses what is foolish, weak, low and despised (I Cor. 1:27-28) to proclaim His gospel to others, so that it is obvious that the glorious power within must be from God (2 Cor. 4:7).

So we see that DIVINE POWER is available to those who will acknowledge that they are weak and unable to witness for Jesus in their own strength.

STUDY 4

CHRISTIAN LIVING

QUESTIONS

DAY 1   Chapter 5:1-9.

a) What word does Paul use to denote: (1) our physical bodies? (2) our spiritual bodies?

not permanent — tent *easily uprooted*   *permanent* — house *established*

b) What affirmations does Paul repeat in 4:1, 16; 5:6, 8.

intermediate state between death & resurrection — a disembodied state but NOT limbo

v.5 - Spirit-deposit guaranteeing our inheritance

i Jn3:2&3 now we are children of God

2Co4:18 seen-temporary, unseen-eternal

DAY 2   Chapter 5:9; John 8:29; Romans 15:1-3.

a) What should be every Christian's aim in life?

To please God   Rom 6 Dead to Sin, Alive in Christ   Ro8:1 No condemnation for those who are in Christ Jesus

1Jn5:3 this is love for God: to obey His commands

b) Is it yours?

c) What do we read about Christ in these verses?

Jn8:29   That God was with Him & He always did what pleased Him

Ro5:13   that He did not please Himself

DAY 3   Chapter 5:10-13; Romans 14:10-12.

a) What reason is put forward here for pleasing God in our daily lives?

That all will face judgement for their life's work

b) How would you explain 'the fear of the Lord'? (v. 11) See also Proverbs 1:7.

The knowledge that you are accountable to Him for your wrong doing and that out of love He will discipline you accordingly.   JOB5:17

PRV13:24 'don't spare the rod

DAY 4   Chapter 5:14-15.

(Can you say these verses from memory?)

a) How can we let God's love control us? (See Rom. 6:13; 12:1, 2.) — Renew the mind..

choice / free will - to sin or not to sin that is the question

offer ourselves to God

Rom8:5 We become what we spend our time focusing on: if we focus on sin — sin results,

if we focus on God - righteousness results

Continuing to sin —
See Rom7 esp.v17-20
1Jn1:8-10
1Jn2:1-2
* 1Jn3:9 *

QUESTIONS (contd.)

b) Can you share with the others in your group any way in which Christ controls your daily life? *the desire to love & serve*

DAY 5 *Chapter 5:16-17, Ephesians 4:22-24.*
a) Do you agree with verse 17? Is it true personally?

b) How do you know? *– CONVICTION OF SIN LEADING TO REPENT*
2Tim 2:19 'The Lord knows those who are His, *him is we obey his commands*
1Jn2:3 we know that we have come to know
1 Jn 1:6

1Jn 3:10

c) What does it mean to be 'in Christ'? Read 2 Corinthians 13:5.
To be born again   to have the Holy Spirit in us

DAY 6 *Chapter 5:18, 19; 1 Peter 2:24.*
a) How did God reconcile us to Himself?
Through Christ Jesus

b) Because of this, what benefit do we have? and what responsibility?
Reconciled to God to share this message of how to be reconciled with others

DAY 7 *Chapter 5:20, 21.*
As an 'ambassador for Christ' yourself, consider these questions.
a) Does an ambassador fail to promote his country's interests?

b) Does he give his own opinion on a controversial issue?

c) Does he act on his own authority?

d) Does he find it strange to take orders from his government?

e) Does he remain for long periods out of touch with his government?

NOTES

Reading and discussing this will benefit everyone.

I wish we could spend a whole term on this marvellous chapter 5! There is so much to learn from it, and the jewels we are searching for are thick on the ground here.

Verses 1-5 **A Christian's attitude to dying**
A sure hope (vv. 1, 5, 6, 7 'we know').
An earnest longing for what is more glorious and more permanent.

Verses 6-10 **A Christian's attitude to living**
Always being of good courage.
Walking by faith.
Pleasing God by what we do.
Knowing that we will be judged later by how we live now.

Verses 11-13 **A Christian's attitude to people in general**
Seeking to win them for Christ.
Being a good example.
Having their welfare at heart.

Verses 14-15 **A Christian's attitude to his Lord**
Living for Jesus a life that is true,
Striving to please Him in all that I do,
Yielding allegiance, gladhearted and free,
This is the pathway of blessing for me.

Living for Jesus who died in my place,
Bearing on Calvary my sin and disgrace,
Such love constrains me to answer His call,
Follow His leading and give Him my all.

Some translations of verse 14 are – 'Christ's love controls us now' (LB); 'For the love of Christ constraineth us' (AV) (constrain – urge with irresistible power); 'We are ruled by the love of Christ' (GNB); 'For the love of Christ leaves us no choice' (NEB); 'The very spring of our actions is the love of Christ' (Phillips).

John Hunter summed up these verses well when he said – 'He died that I might live, now I must die so that He can live'.

Verses 16-21 A Christian's attitude to other Christians.

Seeing them as God sees them, that is new creations with sins forgiven. They are in Christ, as he is in Christ.

Does the love of Christ really control your attitude to dying? living? people in general? Christ your Lord? and other Christians?

Be sure you can say verses 14 and 15 by heart. Ask your leader for help if you need it.

STUDY 5

HOLINESS

QUESTIONS

1 Pet 3: 12-14
— situation with sharon cross

DAY 1 *Chapter 5:20; 6:1, 2.*
a) How did God speak to you through last week's study?
Reminded of the importance of obedience
Treasures in heaven - christ, love; other people
b) There is a note of urgency in today's verses. Why is this?
Now is the time of salvation and we don't know
how long this time has left

DAY 2 *Chapter 6:3-5.*
a) Why did Paul feel it was important that his conduct was beyond
reproach? Read 2 Corinthians 11:24-28. *ministry not discredited 6:3*

the church puts people off

b) What quality did God bring out in Paul through his sufferings?
Humility   Patient endurance   dependance on God
aware of how weak
he was

DAY 3 *Chapter 6:6-7; Galatians 5:22, 23.*
a) Test yourself by the qualities listed here. Which ones do you feel
you lack, and should pray for?

b) What enables us to produce these qualities?

DAY 4 *Chapter 6:8-13.*
Paul was often misunderstood. List the ideas the world had about him,
then how God considered him (which was what he really was).

2 CORINTHIANS • STUDY 5 • HOLINESS

QUESTIONS (contd.)

DAY 5   *Chapter 6:14-16.*

'I'm sure it's God's will for me to marry him, although he's not a Christian.'

a) Would you agree with a Christian girl who said this? Why, or why not?

b) In what other ways might a Christian be tempted to 'be teamed with those who don't love the Lord'?

DAY 6   *Chapter 6:16-18; I Corinthians 3:16, 17; Hosea 2:23.*

a) What promises does God give to us if we are 'holy', that is, set apart for His use?

b) What does verse 17 mean in your life?

DAY 7   *Chapter 7:1; Hebrews 12:14; I Thessalonians 4:3-7.*

a) What is holiness, in practical terms?

b) What command does God give us in Leviticus 20:7, 8?

NOTES

Are you encouraging one another to be holy?

'Sanctification' is the twin word for holiness. The Presbyterian catechism says, 'Sanctification is the work of God's free grace, whereby we are renewed in the whole man after the image of God and are enabled more and more to die unto sin, and to live unto righteousness.'

In chapter 6, Paul urges his readers to accept God's salvation, freely offered in Jesus Christ, NOW. If there are any reading these notes who have not yet accepted Jesus Christ as their personal Saviour, the call comes clearly to you today.

NOW is the accepted time, don't put it off any longer.

A life of holiness is impossible without the Spirit of God living in your heart.

Verses 3-5   **Holiness in action**

Paul endured: internal conflicts – pressures, hardships, anxieties; external conflicts – beatings, imprisonment, riots; self-imposed disciplines – hard work, sleepless nights, fasting (or being too busy to eat).

Verses 6-7   **Fruits of holiness**

Qualities of mind – purity, knowledge, endurance.
Qualities of heart – kindness, the Holy Spirit, genuine love.
Qualities for preaching the gospel – truthful speech, the power of God, weapons of righteousness.

Verses 8-13   **Unrecognised holiness**

Our moral conduct must be consistent with our message. What we say must not contradict what we do. However, it is not unusual for a Christian to be misunderstood, and Paul gives here the contrast between what he really is and what other people think he is.

Verses 14-16   **The common sense of holiness**

By five striking questions all anticipating answers in the negative, Paul shows us that oil and water don't mix. How ridiculous to think that light and darkness can be in the same place! If we switch a light on, the darkness goes. How equally ridiculous to think that a believer can live as one with an unbeliever!

Verses 16-18   **God's promise to a holy people**

From the days when Moses set up the Tabernacle at God's command, to our own day God has required a place set apart so that He can dwell among his people. The Tabernacle had its sanctuary, the Temple its Holy of Holies, and under the Christian dispensation God chooses to dwell in the hearts of His people.

Have you realised what a solemn and thrilling truth this is? God's promise is that He will live in us. Surely the need for holiness in our lives is obvious.

Chapter 7:1   Appeal for holiness

So the appeal comes to you and me, 'let us cleanse ourselves' (RSV), 'let us turn away from everything wrong' (LB), 'let us keep clear of anything that smirches body or soul' (Phillips).

The standard is high – but God set the standard!

[handwritten annotations:]

Attack
Defend
Counter Attack } negative

Forgive
Do not bear grudges.

Encouragement
Invitation
Affirm that is Good 7:13
Follow up afterwards 12:16

Stand your ground.

Be Gentle after being firm
7:4
7:15
13:11-13

Use discipline when
all else fails rebuke
with caution as it is
to help not hurt.

Time Bold 7:9,10:2
Know Facts 11:22-27

Speak
as christ
would
10:3
0:12
13
2:19

STUDY 6

JOY AND SORROW

QUESTIONS

Remember – the key to growth is daily study.

- strong enough to die for them

DAY 1 Chapter 7:2-4.

What were Paul's feelings for the Christians at Corinth?

openness- honest 7:14; 8:21

Read also 6:11-13. Can you learn anything from these two passages that would be helpful in making up a quarrel?

DAY 2 Chapter 7:5; chapter 2:12-13.

a) How did Paul feel when he came to Macedonia?

- harassed, anxious about Titus

b) Why was this? (See Background Notes page 6.) *conflicts internal fears*

DAY 3 Chapter 7:6-8; chapter 1:3-4.

a) How did God comfort him? *by bringing Titus to him and by the news he brought*

b) What effect did the letter have on the Corinthians?

DAY 4 Chapter 7:9-12.

a) What are the results of godly sorrow? *repentance leading to salvation leaves no regret*

b) What does worldly grief produce? (v. 10) *death*

guilt

ISAIAH 6:7

[left margin handwritten:]
Marks of:
earnestness
eagerness to clear ones self
indignation, alarm
longing, concern, readiness
for JUSTICE

QUESTIONS (contd.)

DAY 5 *Chapter 7:13-16; Romans 12:15.*
What else made Paul rejoice? - *how happy Titus was*

Think of someone you can rejoice with this week. Visit and encourage them by sharing their joy.

DAY 6 *Chapter 8:1-2.*
a) What had the churches in Macedonia been going through at this time?

b) In spite of this, Paul says their abundance of joy and their extreme poverty resulted in ....

DAY 7 *Chapter 8:3-5.*
Can you spot five interesting things about their giving?

NOTES

Life is a mixture of joys and sorrows. Paul found this and our study today gives us a glimpse into his very heart.

What kind of things made Paul happy?

His love for the Christians in Corinth (7:4).
Hearing about their spiritual growth (7:7).
The results of his own obedience to the Lord in sending the letter of rebuke (7:9).
Someone else's joy (7:13).
The fact that the Corinthians had vindicated the trust he put in them (7:16).
The way God was touching the hearts of the Christians in Macedonia (8:1).

What kind of things make *you* happy?

How did Paul regard sorrow?

One of the precious verses in this passage tells us 'For God sometimes uses sorrow in our lives to help us turn away from sin and seek eternal life. We should never regret his sending it' (ch. 7:10, LB).

Phillips translates the last sentence, 'You can look back now and see how the hand of God was in that sorrow'. Isn't this very true?

Let us remember this when next we feel sad or downhearted and ask, 'Lord, what do you want to teach me through this experience?'

'The Loom of Time' by Eleanor Leah Woods

1. Man's life is laid in the loom of time
   To a pattern he does not see,
   While the Weaver works and the shuttles fly
   Till the dawn of Eternity.

2. Some shuttles are filled with silver threads
   And some with threads of gold
   While often but the darker hues
   Are all that they may hold.

3. But the Weaver watches with skilful eye
   Each shuttle fly to and fro
   And sees the pattern so deftly wrought
   As the loom moves sure and slow.

4. God surely planned the pattern;
   Each thread, the dark and fair,
   Is chosen by His master skill
   And placed in the web with care.

5. He only knows its beauty
   And guides the shuttles which hold
   The threads so unattractive
   As well as the threads of gold.

6. Not till each loom is silent
   And the shuttles cease to fly,
   Will God reveal the pattern
   And explain the reason why —

7. The dark threads were as needful
   In the Weaver's skilful hand
   As the threads of gold and silver
   For the pattern which He planned.

(handwritten top) Means $1,000 available to me
$500 of that accounted for - food, clothes, etc.
$500 able to give
$600 more than able - I will have to make a sacrifice!

STUDY 7

CHRISTIAN GIVING

QUESTIONS

(handwritten) GRACIOUSLY — not uncertain as to the amount but certain

HOW TO GIVE
(handwritten) — not reluctantly but cheerfully — From what you have - not out of debt

DAY 1 2 Corinthians 8:1-8; 9:7; Exodus 35:5. —
Both by example and command in which three ways does God's word
tells us to give? *(handwritten)* v.5 1st to the Lord

(handwritten) v.3 as much as they were able   v.8 sincerely - shown by earnestness
NOT all that they had   even beyond that

DAY 2 1 Corinthians 16:2; 2 Corinthians 8:10-15.
From these verses find two ways God wants us to give.
(handwritten) v.11 eagerly, willingly, completely, according to your means

WHY WE GIVE
(handwritten) poor - despised rejected   the
rich - grace Eph 2:7   riches of His Grace

DAY 3 2 Corinthians 8:9; John 3:16.
a) Why did Jesus become poor? *(handwritten)* - For our sake that we might become rich

(handwritten) Rich
R 12:15 - not in abundance of possessions - Lk 12:21

(handwritten) Eph 3:8 the unsearchable riches of Christ

b) Why did God give His son to die?
(handwritten) Eph 3:11 & 12

(handwritten right margin) Poverty rejected despised   Rich recognised powerful esteemed accepted

DAY 4 Matthew 10:8; Luke 6:38; Acts 20:35. *(handwritten)* It is more blessed to give than to receive.
What three things did Jesus say about giving?
(handwritten) Freely you have received freely give   Give and it will be given to you

HOW MUCH SHOULD WE GIVE?
(handwritten) Tithe & offerings

DAY 5 Leviticus 27:30-34; Malachi 3:8. —
(handwritten) Tithe
a) How much were the Jews taught to give?
(handwritten) 10% belongs to the Lord

QUESTIONS (contd.)

b) What is the Christian's obligation in giving today?

DAY 6 *2 Corinthians 9:6-10; Philippians 4:18-19.*
a) Write verse 8 briefly in your own words.

b) Will giving to the Lord's work leave us short?

v.8 we will have all we need
Ph4:19 —

DAY 7 *2 Corinthians 9:11-15; Malachi 3:10.*
a) What happens when we give the Bible way?

b) If we are faithful givers what does Malachi say will happen?

God's blessing will be poured out.

NOTES

Christian giving – this is something very practical and it is a personal challenge to each one of us. As a result of preparing this study, I have realised that the Lord wants me to increase my giving to His work. As the cost of living rises, so the level of my giving should rise too.

May He speak to each one of us and touch our hearts!

Below are some pertinent comments on giving which may be lined up with the seven days of questions we are discussing together. Ponder them slowly.

1. It is not the gift of the lover that counts, but the love of the giver.
2. Is the amount due to God's work equally as important as that bill that has to be paid?
3. First plan to give as much as you can comfortably afford – and then increase the figure until it becomes a sacrifice.
4. God does not measure the gift by its size, but by what we have left when we have given.
5. Only when we have given one tenth to God (our duty) can we then, over and above that, make a real offering to Him.
6. If you are a giver, God will see to it that you always have something to give.
7. Christians have no idea of what they are missing, in terms of enjoyment and enrichment until they have learned to give on God's terms.

Stephen Olford in 'The Grace of Giving' says:

'Paul's conception of giving is a lofty one. To him, giving is a grace, a ministry of the Holy Spirit inwrought in personal experience and outworked in practical expression.'

A verse to learn: 2 Corinthians 8:9.

STUDY 8

BOASTING ABOUT THE LORD

QUESTIONS

DAY 1   *Chapter 10:1-2; Matthew 11:29.*
a) What characteristics of Christ did Paul boast about?

b) What did his critics say about him?

DAY 2   *Chapter 10:3-4; Ephesians 6:10-13; Zechariah 4:6.*
a) What do you think are the 'weapons' referred to here?

b) What can these weapons do?

DAY 3   *Chapter 10:5-6; Jeremiah 9:23, 24.*
a) What words used here continue the imagery of fighting a war?

b) What things do people often boast about?

DAY 4   *Chapter 10:7-9; 1 Corinthians 9:1-2.*
a) Paul's critics claimed he was not a true apostle. How did he answer that accusation?

b) What gave Paul confidence to continue his work, even in the face of opposition? (Mark 1:22)

QUESTIONS (contd.)

DAY 5 *Chapter 10:10-12; I Corinthians 2:1-5.*
a) What did the critics say about his letters, and about the impression he made in person?

b) Did he say more in his letters than he had the courage to carry out?

DAY 6 *Chapter 10:13-16; Galatians 6:14. (See also Phillips translations).*
a) In what way did God limit Paul's boasting?

b) What was Paul's ambition in evangelism? (Rom. 15:20).

DAY 7 *Chapter 10:17-18; Jeremiah 9:23-24.*
a) What have you got to boast about?

b) What is the only commendation that is important to the Christian?

NOTES

'So what about these wise men, these scholars, these brilliant debaters of this world's great affairs? God has made them all look foolish and shown their wisdom to be useless nonsense. For God in his wisdom saw to it that the world would never find God through human brilliance, and then he stepped in and saved all those who believed his message, which the world calls foolish and silly' (I Cor. 1:20, 21, LB).

Men fortify themselves against the gospel with their intellect and will.

To win others, we must use the weapons God has prepared. Do we do this, or do we try to fight using our own resources?

Remember that God's mighty weapons are able to destroy the devil's stronghold (2 Cor. 10:4).

Having pulled down the stronghold, Christ seeks to take every thought captive to obey Him.

Criticism Against Paul	Paul's Boast
'You don't belong to Christ' (v. 7).	'I stand on the authority of Christ' (v. 8).
'Your letters are severe and strong, you are weak' (v. 10).	'There is no difference between what I write and what I will do' (v. 11).
'You're not as good as we are' (v. 12).	'God controls my work and witness' (v. 13).
'We've never heard a worse preacher (v. 10).	'I'm not ashamed of the Gospel' (Rom. 1:16)

Criticism hurts ... hurts our pride? How do we react?

After Paul and Barnabas' first missionary journey, during which they saw many people turning to the Lord, 'they gathered the church (in Antioch) together and declared all that GOD had done with them, and how HE had opened a door of faith to the Gentiles' (Acts 14:27 RSV). Paul, writing about himself to the Christians at Rome, said, 'For I will not venture to speak of anything except what Christ has wrought through me' (Rom. 15:18 RSV).

It was not by chance that the theme song at 'Billy Graham' Crusades was –

'To God be the glory, great things HE has done.'

Verse to learn: 2 Corinthians 10:17.

STUDY 9

THE PRICELESS GAIN OF KNOWING CHRIST

QUESTIONS

To understand Chapter 11, we must recognise that it is an outburst by Paul:

(1) Of his jealous love in the Lord for the Christians at Corinth,

(2) Of his 'sanctified scorn' against those who were 'preaching another Jesus' to them.

This accounts for the vehemence of his writing in places and for the fact that he boasts about himself, which normally he would not do.

DAY 1   *Chapter 11:1-6; Ephesians 5:25-27; Revelation 21:2.*
a) To what is the Church likened in these verses?

— pure virgin — wife   — bride

b) What was Paul afraid would happen?

deception - led astray

DAY 2   *Chapter 11:7-12.*
a) How was Paul supported while he was at Corinth?

by other churches

b) When he was in need, who came to his aid? (Remember them from 8:1, 2?)   *Macedonians*

DAY 3   *Chapter 11:4, 13-20.*
a) What words are used to describe the men who were masquerading as Christian teachers?   *deceitful workmen*
preachers   false apostles   Satan-angel of light

b) What had they been doing at Corinth as a result of their counterfeit preaching? (v. 20)   *enslavery   exploitation*

QUESTIONS (contd.)

DAY 4   *Chapter 11:21-23.*

a) What four things did the false teachers boast about?

Hebrews, Israelites, Abraham's descendants, servants of Christ facing suffering and hardship

b) How does Paul meet these claims?

He is too

DAY 5   *Chapter 11:23-27; Galatians 6:17.*

Make a list of the physical punishments mentioned here and another of the hazards and hardships he had been through.

DAY 6   *Chapter 11:28-29.*

a) What else did Paul have to endure?

b) How was this demonstrated in practical terms? (v. 29)

DAY 7   *Chapter 11:30-33; Acts 9:23-25.*

a) What kind of things does Paul feel he can legitimately boast about?

b) What humiliation at the beginning of his service for God does he still remember?

NOTES

This chapter, and indeed the whole book we are studying, gives us a glimpse of what it meant for the Apostle Paul to be a Christian.

Before his conversion, he was –

(a) A Jew from Tarsus in Cilicia, a citizen of a wealthy city (Acts 21:39).

(b) A Roman citizen by birth, implying status in the community (Acts 22:27-28).

(c) Of pure Hebrew stock, of the tribe of Benjamin, from which the first king of Israel had been appointed (I Sam. 10:20-24).

(d) A religious man with a good reputation, who lived a good, blameless life (Phil. 3:5, 6).

(e) A well-educated man. As the son of a devout Pharisee, he would have begun to read the Scriptures at five years old, and continued his education under the Rabbis, concluding with a 'university' course under the instruction of the illustrious 'professor' Gamaliel in Jerusalem (Acts 22:3). Not only did he study, but he was top of the class! (Gal. 1:14)

(f) Skilled in a trade, as every honourable Jew was. Paul was a tentmaker (Acts 18:3).

After his conversion – well, we have been reading something of his life story after he decided to follow Christ. It is quite a contrast, isn't it?

Did Paul think back longingly to the days of wealth, comfort, position, security and intellectual stimulation?

Let him tell us in his own words, written near the end of his life.

'Yet every advantage that I had gained I considered loss for Christ's sake. Yes, and I look upon everything as loss compared with the overwhelming gain of knowing Christ Jesus my Lord. For His sake I did in actual fact suffer the loss of everything, but I considered it useless rubbish compared with being able to win Christ. For now my place is in him, and I am not dependent upon any of the self-achieved righteousness of the Law. God has given me that genuine righteousness which comes from faith in Christ. How changed are my ambitions! Now I long to know Christ and the power shown by his resurrection: now I long to share his suffering, even to die as he died, so that I may perhaps attain, as he did, the resurrection from the dead' (Phil. 3:7-11, Phillips).

A verse to learn: Philippians 3:8 (first half).

STUDY 10

'MY GRACE IS SUFFICIENT'

QUESTIONS

Is your study time each day becoming a must?
Read all of chapters 12 and 13 on the first day. This week we are going to concentrate on chapter 12:1-10 for our study. As there is only one question a day, take time to think carefully about this passage.

DAY 1   *Chapter 12:2-4, 7.*
Paul is speaking about himself. How does he describe the spiritual experience he had?

DAY 2   *Chapter 12:7.*
How does Paul describe the irritating thing (whatever it actually was) which harassed, or buffeted him?

DAY 3   *Chapter 12:8; Mark 14:32-41.*
What was the difference between Paul's prayers and Christ's?

Similarities
3x
take it away
accepted circumstance
present, future
asked for God's will
consequence of it being taken away would effect Paul only whereas consequence for Christ would have affected the whole world

DAY 4   *Chapter 12:9; Philippians 4:13; Romans 8:35-37.*
What great principle of faith did Paul learn?

Complete dependency upon Christ

DAY 5   *Chapter 12:9, 13:4 (Living Bible).*
Do you find the answer to your human limitations in these verses?

What practically can we do to live this way?

Prov 3:5

WITHOUT ME YOU CAN DO NOTHING > Eternal Consequence

QUESTIONS (contd.)

DAY 6 *Chapter 12:9-10 (Look up several versions including the New English Bible.)*
How do we see a change in Paul's attitude here?

DAY 7 *Chapter 12:10, 13:8-9.*
How do you explain the contradictory statement, 'When I am weak, then I am strong'?

Something to think about.
What can we learn from this passage about answers to prayer?

Can you think of any examples you could share?

My grace is sufficient – the way may seem long,
But yet in your weakness My strength is made strong,
In things that oppress you, perhaps cause you pain,
I'll give you the victory again and again.

My grace is sufficient – life's burdens press sore,
But I am thy portion, rejoice evermore;
For burdens will bring you so close to My side,
That leaning upon Me, in peace you'll abide!

My grace is sufficient – what more would you ask?
I give, with the vision, the strength for the task.
'Tis not yours to question My pleasure to use
A weak earthen vessel, if this I should choose.

My grace is sufficient – a boundless supply
Is yours for the taking, if you will draw nigh,
Grace all-sufficient to meet every need,
For I am the Saviour, thy Keeper indeed.

– i.e. I can do my job perfectly well in the worlds eyes without it having any eternal consequence.

NOTES

Surely this section is the richest and most beautiful jewel that lies waiting to be appropriated in this wonderful letter. It gives us the answer to a question that every human being asks, 'What is the secret of meeting sorrow and suffering?'

Let us follow Paul here, step by step, and find the secret for ourselves.

The Spiritual Experience
Fourteen years back from the writing of this letter takes us to the time just before Paul set off on his first missionary journey (Acts 13:1-3). The Lord saw fit to grant him this 'mountain-top experience', perhaps to strengthen him for what lay ahead, even as Christ was strengthened on the Mount of Transfiguration. (Tyndale Commentary, pages 170-2 is helpful here.)

The Thorn in the Flesh
Have you ever had a thorn in your finger? How irritating and painful it can be. Numerous suggestions have been made as to what Paul's thorn was. Some think he may have had trouble with his eyes, others think it may have been recurring malaria, or epilepsy, yet others would see it as a spiritual 'thorn' – temptation to despair or doubt, something of 'the flesh' as the word is used in Romans 8:7-9.

Some suggest that perhaps the opposition that dogged his footsteps is meant. Surely the most heartening thing about the 'thorn' is that we do not know what it was! Therefore, if we have any physical ailment or handicap, any persistent frustration, or indeed any circumstances or situation that we long to be rid of – we can identify with Paul here. What matters is not what the 'thorn' is, but how we react to it.

The Purpose of the Thorn
'To keep me from being unduly elated by the magnificence of such revelations' (NEB).

'In order to prevent my becoming absurdly conceited' (Phillips).

'God was afraid I might be puffed up by them' (LB).

Yes, but surely there was a deeper purpose. How else would Paul learn the secret of overcoming a nagging, persistent problem? Consider how many people have shared this secret since Paul's day, through reading this letter.

The Prayer that seemed Unheard
He prayed – but with a preconceived idea of what the answer should be. It was quite clear to him that, as the 'thorn' was hindering his effectiveness for God, it had to go. 'Lord, I could serve you much better if you would remove this pressure ... that person ... this unpleasant thing. So please take it away.'

Does that sound like, 'Not my will, but Thine?' Notice that Paul asked three times and then he stopped asking and listened!

What are you going to study next?

ANSWER GUIDE

The following pages contain an Answer Guide. It is recommended that answers to the questions be attempted before turning to this guide. It is only a guide and the answers given should not be treated as exhaustive.

GUIDE TO STUDY 1

DAY 1 a) The Father of our Lord Jesus Christ, the Father of mercies, the God of all comfort.
b) So that we may be able to comfort others in trouble.
c) Personal.

DAY 2 a) To share in someone's sufferings brings the added blessing of sharing in their comfort.
b) Utterly, unbearably crushed, despairing even of life itself.

DAY 3 a) Rely on God.
b) Pray for him.

DAY 4 a) In all his dealings he was pure and sincere (Living Bible).
b) The grace of God.

DAY 5 a) They say 'yes' when they mean 'no'.
b) Personal.
c) Personal answers to second question. Examples are:
God promises peace (Isa. 26:3). We have peace through Jesus (Rom. 5:1).
God promises One who will set the captives free (Isa. 61:1). Jesus fulfilled this (Luke 4:18-21).
God promises a new covenant (Jer. 31:33). Jesus proclaimed this (1 Cor. 11:25).

DAY 6 a) He didn't want to make them sad by having to rebuke them.
b) He says it almost broke his heart, and he wept over it.

DAY 7 a) One of discipline, forgiveness, comfort and an expression of love.
b) (How) By God's authority.
(Why) For the good of the church at Corinth, and to keep Satan from gaining an advantage.

GUIDE TO STUDY 2

DAY 1 a) Titus.
b) The practical nature of the letter.

DAY 2 a) Christ leads us or uses us (He must be in control), and works through us (His power).
b) To diffuse the fragrance of Christ to Christians and non-Christians alike.

DAY 3 a) The work of the Spirit in their lives had brought about a change which was evident to all. They were Christ's stamp of approval on the ministry of Paul.
b) The old covenant was written on tablets of stone, the new was a change of heart.

DAY 4 a) His confidence was in God alone (not himself) and he knew he had been sent by God to bring God's message to others. God had blessed his ministry among them (Acts 9:15).
b) Because the law demanded perfect obedience if eternal life was to be obtained by it (Gal. 3:10) and sinners found this impossible (Rom. 3:20).

DAY 5 a) Moses' face shone because he had been talking with God.
b) The splendour of the new covenant (because of its nature – it brings righteousness) must surpass the other.

DAY 6 a) The fading of the splendour (Moses), the opposite being the permanence and increase of the glory (see v. 18).
b) They heard the words, but did not understand the true meaning.
c) When a person turns to the Lord.

DAY 7 a) Prayer, Bible Study, Worship, keeping our minds fixed on Him (read Phil. 4:8).
b) We are changed – inwardly and outwardly – and grow more like Jesus.
Notes on the word 'beholding' or 'reflecting' in verse 18. There may be queries regarding different translations, or this may not come up at all in the study.

GUIDE TO STUDY 3

DAY 1
a) Because he has such a splendid ministry of the new covenant to proclaim and it has been entrusted to Him by God.
b) The gospel of Jesus Christ, the Son of God; His atoning death and resurrection.

DAY 2
a) Because Satan has blinded them to the truth.
b) They are 'lost', 'on the road to eternal death', 'perishing'.

DAY 3
a) He is the creator, even of light, and has mighty power; He enlightens the minds of all true Christians through a saving knowledge of Jesus.
b) Christ.
c) Yes.
Personal. (Leaders, help others to share how they came to know Christ, and draw out the metaphor of physical light and spiritual light).

DAY 4
a) The light of the knowledge of the glory of God.
b) To show that it is from God and to share it with others.
c) Because when we are not trusting in our own abilities, we depend completely on Him, and His power can flow through us.

DAY 5

Weakness:	Power:
Afflicted,	Not crushed,
perplexed,	not driven to despair,
persecuted,	not forsaken,
struck down,	not destroyed,
carrying in the body,	the life of Jesus manifested
the death of Jesus,	in our bodies,
death at work in us.	life in you.

DAY 6
a) Because even death held no terrors for him, as it would be only the beginning of life in the presence of his Lord.
b) God's power in raising Jesus from the dead.

DAY 7
a) Bible reading, prayer, thinking about the things of God.
b) Material things come to an end, spiritual values last for ever (I Cor. 13:8).
c) The unseen, eternal things.

GUIDE TO STUDY 4

DAY 1
(a) Tent.
(b) House, Home, Building.
'We do not lose heart' or 'we are of good courage' or 'we are confident'.

DAY 2
a) To please Christ in everything.
b) Personal.
c) He did not please Himself, He pleased the Father.

DAY 3
a) Because one day we shall be judged according to how we have lived.
b) Awe and reverence for a Mighty Creator, coupled with a fervent desire not to hurt or displease Him, because we love Him.

DAY 4
a) Yield our lives to Him, present our bodies to Him day by day.
b) Personal.

DAY 5
a) Personal.
b) 'In Christ' is one of the ways in which Paul describes a Christian, i.e. one who has Christ living in him.
c) I John 5:12; Galatians 2:20; John 15:4.

DAY 6
a) Through Christ's death on the Cross.
b) Our sins are blotted out; we are to tell others this message.

DAY 7
Personal.

GUIDE TO STUDY 5

DAY 1 a) Personal.
b) Because God's offer is open NOW, and no one knows for how much longer.

DAY 2 a) He didn't want to put any obstacle in the way of a person seeking the Lord.
b) Endurance.

DAY 3 a) Personal.
b) The power of God, the Holy Spirit.

DAY 4

World	God
Dishonour	Honour
Ill repute (criticism)	Good repute (commendation)
Impostors (liars)	True (honest)
Unknown	Known
As good as dead	Very much alive
Punished (injured)	Kept from death
Sorrowful	Rejoicing
Poor	Rich spiritually
Owning nothing	Possessing everything

DAY 5 a) No. Because the definite command in verse 14 forbids it. Those who honour God, He will honour; and to find His best for us in life, we dare not go against His commands.
b) Partnership in business; to compromise one's code of conduct in order to be accepted socially; to lower one's standards for financial gain; young people getting into wrong company.

DAY 6 a) He will live with us and walk among us.
He will be our God and we shall be His people (v. 16).
He will be a Father to us and we shall be His children (v. 18).
In other words, an intimate and close relationship will exist between us and God.
b) Personal. (The Christian must be prepared to be different.)

DAY 7 a) Cleansing from every defilement of body and spirit (2 Cor. 7:1), living a clean life (Heb. 12:14 LB), high moral conduct, clean-minded (1 Thess. 4:3-7).
b) To consecrate ourselves to the Lord and to be holy as He is holy.

GUIDE TO STUDY 6

DAY 1 a) They were dear to his heart, he had confidence in them, he was proud of them, they were a source of comfort and joy to him.
b) An expression of genuine love for the other party, a longing for a restored relationship, an openness and a clear conscience, a willingness to take the first step.

DAY 2 a) Anxious and fearful (see also NEB 2 Cor. 7:5).
b) Because he had sent a letter of rebuke to the Corinthians, with Titus, and was waiting to hear how it was received.

DAY 3 a) By bringing Titus to meet him, and by the good news which Titus carried.
b) It grieved them.

DAY 4 a) Repentance, a turning to God, eagerness to get rid of sin.
b) Death.

DAY 5 The fact that Titus rejoiced in his visit to Corinth.

DAY 6 a) A severe test of affliction (hard times).
b) An overflow of giving to others. They gave lavishly with an open-hand.

DAY 7 They gave:
    (1) What they could afford.
    (2) Beyond their means.
    (3) Of their own free will.
    (4) They looked upon it as a favour to be able to contribute.
    (5) They first gave themselves to the Lord.

GUIDE TO STUDY 7

DAY 1   1) Cheerfully.
2) Generously.
3) Eagerly.

DAY 2   1) Regularly.
2) Sensibly or systematically.

DAY 3   a) He became poor for our sakes in order for us to become rich.
b) He loved us so much and wanted us to have eternal life.

DAY 4   1) Freely you have received, freely give.
2) Give, and it shall be given unto you.
3) It is more blessed to give than to receive.

DAY 5   a) One Tenth.
b) Proportionate to my income.

DAY 6   a) God is able to provide enough for us.
b) God will supply all our needs.

DAY 7   a) Those in need are helped.
b) The gift 'overflows' in thanksgiving to God.
You will glorify God by your obedience.
Others will pray for you.
God will open up the windows of heaven and pour out a great blessing.

Make sure you watch the time and guide discussion so that all the questions are covered each week. Avoid discussion 'off the point'; deal with queries and doctrinal issues on a person to person basis afterwards.

GUIDE TO STUDY 8

DAY 1
    a) Meekness and gentleness (LB 'I plead gently').
    b) That he was brave at a distance, but afraid when he came to visit.

DAY 2
    a) The Holy Spirit, prayer, God's power, or any listed in Ephesians 6.
    b) Defend us and enable us to overcome evil.

DAY 3
    a) Taking captive (LB 'capture rebels').
    b) Their own wisdom, their own might, their own riches.

DAY 4
    a) He belonged to Christ, he had seen Christ, and the Church in Corinth was a living proof of his genuineness.
    b) The authority of the Lord.

DAY 5
    a) His letters were weighty and powerful, but he was nothing to look at, and was a poor speaker!
    b) No.

DAY 6
    a) He would only boast about the Cross of Christ, and the wonders God had done in human hearts.
    b) To preach the Gospel where no one had preached it before.

DAY 7
    a) Personal.
    b) The Lord's commendation.

GUIDE TO STUDY 9

DAY 1   a) The Bride of Christ.
b) That the Christians would follow false teaching.

DAY 2   a) Churches from other areas supported him.
b) The Macedonian Christians.

DAY 3   a) False apostles, deceitful workmen.
b) Deceiving and taking advantage of the Christians.

DAY 4   They boasted that they were,
a) Hebrews; Jews; Descendants of Abraham; Servants of Christ.
b) He can claim the same credentials, but can also prove that he has suffered for Christ's sake.

DAY 5   Jailed, whipped, lashed, beaten with rods, stoned; faced death, suffered shipwreck and exposure in the open seas, endangered by flooded rivers, in danger at the hands of robbers, Jews, Gentiles, mobs in the cities, privation in the deserts, hunger, cold.

DAY 6   a) The spiritual burden for his converts and churches that they might not suffer or lose out.
b) He felt for each one in their trials and failures.

DAY 7   a) His own weakness, that God might be glorified.
b) How the disciples had to help him escape (in a basket!) over the city wall to protect him from the Jews.

GUIDE TO STUDY 10

DAY 1   Caught up to the third heaven.
Caught up to paradise (NIV).
He heard things which he could not disclose.
Verse 7 refers to 'the abundance of revelations' (RSV), 'the magnificence of such revelations' (NEB), 'these experiences I had were so tremendous' (LB).

DAY 2   A thorn in the flesh. (This is the accurate translation). (Some versions give 'a painful physical ailment' or 'a physical handicap' etc. This is perhaps assuming too much, as some commentators believe it to have been spiritual, with 'the flesh' understood as the old nature).
Also, a messenger of Satan.

DAY 3   Paul asked the Lord to take away the 'thorn'; Christ also asked this, but added, 'not what I will, but what you want'.

DAY 4   That no matter what trials or hardships we have, we can have victory over them through Christ.

DAY 5   a) Yes, we can have the power of Christ in our lives.
b) This is not dependent on how we feel, or what our circumstances are.

DAY 6   He says, 'I'm glad to boast about how weak I am' (LB)
                'I shall therefore *prefer....*' (NEB)
                'I can even enjoy weakness, suffering ... etc.' (Phillips)

DAY 7   As we grow in Christ we find we have to depend on Him to give strength, not just for very obvious disabilities, some may be physical, some temperamental, but for every facet of our human nature. The more we turn our weaknesses over to Him, the more His power comes through in our lives.

THE WORD WORLDWIDE

We first heard of WORD WORLDWIDE over twenty years ago when Marie Dinnen, its founder, shared excitedly about the wonderful way ministry to one needy woman had exploded to touch many lives. It was great to see the Word of God being made central in the lives of thousands of men and women, then to witness the life-changing results of them applying the Word to their circumstances. Over the years the vision for WORD WORLDWIDE has not dimmed in the hearts of those who are involved in this ministry. God is still at work through His Word and in today's self-seeking society, the Word is even more relevant to those who desire true meaning and purpose in life. WORD WORLDWIDE is a ministry of WEC International, an interdenominational missionary society, whose sole purpose is to see Christ known, loved and worshipped by all, particularly those who have yet to hear of His wonderful name. This ministry is a vital part of our work and we warmly recommend the WORD WORLDWIDE 'Geared for Growth' Bible studies to you. We know that as you study His Word you will be enriched in your personal walk with Christ. It is our hope that as you are blessed through these studies, you will find opportunities to help others discover a personal relationship with Jesus. As a mission we would encourage you to work with us to make Christ known to the ends of the earth.

Stewart and Jean Moulds – British Directors, **WEC International**.

A full list of over 50 'Geared for Growth' studies can be obtained from:

John and Ann Edwards
5 Louvaine Terrace, Hetton-le-Hole, Tyne & Wear, DH5 9PP
Tel. 0191 5262803 Email: rhysjohn.edwards@virgin.net

Anne Jenkins
2 Windermere Road, Carnforth, Lancs., LA5 9AR
Tel. 01524 734797 Email: anne@jenkins.abelgratis.com

UK Website: www.gearedforgrowth.co.uk

Christian Focus Publications

publishes books for all ages

Our mission statement –

STAYING FAITHFUL

In dependence upon God we seek to help make His infallible word, the Bible, relevant. Our aim is to ensure that the Lord Jesus Christ is presented as the only hope to obtain forgiveness of sin, live a useful life and look forward to heaven with Him.

REACHING OUT

Christ's last command requires us to reach out to our world with His gospel. We seek to help fulfil that by publishing books that point people towards Jesus and help them develop a Christ-like maturity. We aim to equip all levels of readers for life, work, ministry and mission.

Books in our adult range are published in three imprints.

Christian Focus contains popular works including biographies, commentaries, basic doctrine, and Christian living. Our children's books are also published in this imprint.

Mentor focuses on books written at a level suitable for Bible College and seminary students, pastors, and other serious readers; the imprint includes commentaries, doctrinal studies, examination of current issues, and church history.

Christian Heritage contains classic writings from the past.

For details of our titles visit us on our website
www.christianfocus.com

Christian Focus Publications Ltd
Geanies House, Fearn, Tain,
Ross-shire, IV20 ITW, Scotland, United Kingdom.
info@christianfocus.com